The NASTY paSt

By
John Wood

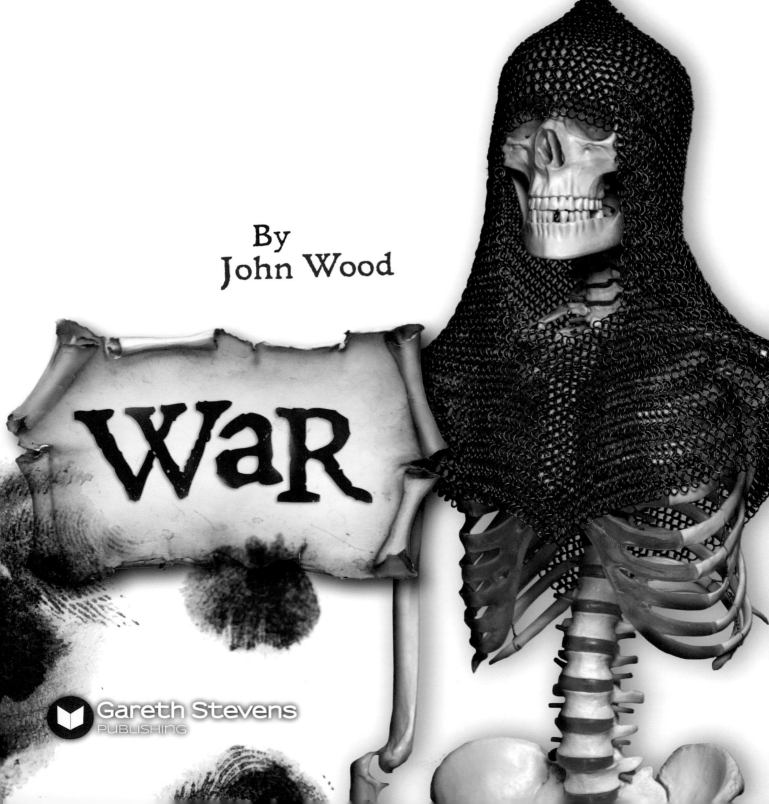

WaR

Gareth Stevens
PUBLISHING

Please visit our website, www.garethstevens.com.
For a free color catalog of all our high-quality books,
call toll free 1-800-542-2595 or fax 1-877-542-2596.

Cataloging-in-Publication Data

Names: Wood, John.
Title: War / John Wood.
Description: New York : Gareth Stevens Publishing, 2020. | Series: The nasty past | Includes glossary and index.
Identifiers: ISBN 9781538252888 (pbk.) | ISBN 9781538252895 (library bound) | ISBN 9781538254165 (6pack)
Subjects: LCSH: War–History–Juvenile literature. | War–Juvenile literature.
Classification: LCC U21.2 W66 2020 | DDC 355.0202'02–dc23

First Edition

Published in 2020 by
Gareth Stevens Publishing
111 East 14th Street, Suite 349
New York, NY 10003

Written by: John Wood
Edited by: Madeline Tyler
Designed by: Dan Scase

Photo credits:
Front cover – ilolab, kaer_stock, Keith Tarrier, Linda George, FXQuadro, Robert B. Miller, Ilkin Zeferli. 4 – salajean,
krugloff. 5 – cosma, Masarik. 6 – Ilkin Zeferli, Charles de Steuben. 7 – Nejron Photo, Baranov E, mollicart.
8 – tomertu, Nejron Photo. 9 – S-F, jorisvo. 10 – Photosebia, Cromagnon, Aleksminyaylo1. 11 – Alexandru Staiu,
Fotokon. 12 – tdemirboga, Jopics. 13 – Stasia04, Jewelzz. 14 – Maestro-0111, Vuk Kostic. 15 – Iren Key, Gilmanshin.
16 – BiblioArchives / LibraryArchives, Oliver Hitchen. 17 – Imperial War Museums, Derek R. Audette, Matt Gibson.
18 – Vladiczech, Everett - Art. 19 – Martina Badini, Darrin Henry. 20 – Everett Historical. 21 – Wellcome Images.
22 – RPBaiao, Mark Van Overmeire. 23 – OSTILL is Franck Camhi, Luis Fco. Pizarro Ruiz. 24 – Adolf Ulrik Wertmüller.
25 – Adwo, www.paris.fr/portail/Culture, Gutzemberg. 26 – Kristian Bell, John Carnemolla. 27 – Paul Broadbent.
28 – Serhii Bobyk, Valeria Vechterova. 29 – Serhii Bobyk, Valery Bocman. 30 – Davide Zanin, Masarik.
Header banners – Novikov Alex. Blood prints – Oksana Mizina. Blood drips – ALEXSTAND. Backgrounds – ilolab,
Groundback Atelier, Krasovski Dmitri, Groundback Atelier. Photo borders – Welena, Krasovski Dmitri.
Stone captions – Philll. Wooden Fact Boxes – My Life Graphic. Blood headings – Olha Burlii. Images are courtesy
of Shutterstock.com. With thanks to Getty Images, Thinkstock Photo and iStockphoto.

Printed in the United States of America

CPSIA compliance information: Batch #CW20GS: For further information contact Gareth Stevens, New York,
New York at 1-800-542-2595.

Contents

Words that look like **THIS** are explained in the glossary on page 31.

A Discovery from the Past

SOMEWHERE, DEEP IN A MUSEUM...

There are secrets underground. It's not all dirt and mud, especially if you know where to look. Buried under all that earth and rock are clues to the past. Whether it's bones, bodies, books, or weapons, each clue tells a story of something that happened a long time ago. And it turns out that these stories can be pretty gruesome...

The people who find and study old, historical objects are called archaeologists (say: ar-kee-ol-uh-jists).

The past was not a nice place to live. People didn't live as long as they do now, and there were plenty of things to kill them before they even reached old age. Towns were dirty, work was brutal, and disease and war were everywhere. Despite all this, people still made pottery and jewelry, built homes and temples, and lived their lives. Some of the things they made are still in the earth with their bones, waiting to be found...

It might not seem like it, but this archaeologist is very, very excited right now.

A NEW STORY

Here in this museum, all sorts of objects are collected so people can learn about history. There are even old skeletons of people who died long ago. Look, here is one! The head is completely separate from the body. The bones are quite old – maybe a few hundred years. This was found in Europe. What happened to this person all that time ago? Who were they, and how were they killed?

The **REMAINS** show that they lost their head at some point. But to find out exactly how this person met their end, you must travel through history. Take a note of each war you learn about and see if any of them might explain our skeleton here. But be careful – the past can be very, very dangerous.

Battle of Tours

In A.D. 732, a large army rode their horses through Gaul, an area of **ANCIENT** Europe. The army was made up of people called Moors; they were **MUSLIMS** from Spain.

Their leader, Abdul al-Rahman, wanted them to take over more of Europe. So far, it had been pretty easy, but that was all about to change.

Between the towns of Tours and Poitiers, Abdul al-Rahman's army suddenly came across another large army that wanted to protect Gaul. It was a group of people called the Franks, and they were led by a man called Charles Martel. However, the Frank army was much smaller, and it didn't have any horses. After a week of standing around in the cold, the Moors decided to attack Charles Martel and his men. However, much to everyone's surprise, they were **DEFEATED**. Abdul al-Rahman was killed, and the rest of his army ran away.

The Battle of Tours is one of the few times in history that an army with horses has lost against an army without horses.

Charles Martel's nickname was "The Hammer." He sounds like a scary guy!

WHAT WENT WRONG FOR THE MOORS?

How did around 80,000 Moors on horses lose against around 30,000 Franks on foot? Did Charles Martel have a secret weapon? Let's find out...

CHARLES MARTEL'S GUIDE TO WINNING REALLY DIFFICULT BATTLES

- *Be sneaky. Martel used back roads to quietly set his army up in the perfect place. This meant he got to choose the battlefield.*

- *Always be at the top of the hill. The Moors had to ride their horses uphill to get to Martel's men. It is hard to attack uphill, and easy to defend downhill.*

- *Use the trees. Abdul al-Rahman's horsemen found it difficult to ride through the forest where Martel and his men were waiting.*

- *Train a good army. Charles Martel didn't force peasants to join his army. He collected lots of money and used it to train skilled soldiers.*

The Battle of Tours might have had big effects on Europe. If Abdul al-Rahman and his men had won, perhaps most people in Europe would have become Muslims instead of **CHRISTIANS**.

The Battle of Hastings

In England, on January 5, 1066, King Edward the Confessor died. Edward did not have any children. As he was dying, he said that he wanted the next king to be Harold Godwinson, who was a **NOBLEMAN**. He was crowned King Harold II the next day. However, there were some people who were very unhappy about this. Harald Hardrada was a Viking who wanted to be king. William of Normandy was a nobleman from France who also wanted to be king. And these men were willing to take the crown by force.

Everyone wanted that shiny golden crown.

The Viking, Harald Hardrada, was attacking from the north, and had conquered the city of York. Harold Godwinson was in the south at the time, expecting an attack by William. He marched his army all the way to York in around 4 days – very, very fast for the time. He killed Hardrada and his men at the Battle of Stamford Bridge.

The Viking, Harald Hardrada, came to England with 300 ships. However, so many people died in the battle that they only needed 24 to go home.

NO TIME FOR CHEERING

Harold II was too busy to celebrate. He had to go south as fast as he could to fight William without a break. William had a very large army and 700 ships. His men had time to rest and get ready for a fight. Harold II, on the other hand, had been marching for two weeks straight by the time he reached the battlefield, a place called Hastings. It was going to be difficult.

William's army was full of trained soldiers. However, many of Harold's soldiers were actually peasants. Some of them fought with pitchforks!

PITCHFORK

THE BATTLE BEGINS!

The fighting lasted most of the day. William's army attacked with arrows and men on horses, while Harold's army defended the top of a hill with a strong wall of shields. Suddenly, William's soldiers seemed like they were running away. Harold II and his men broke their wall of shields and chased after them. However, it was a trick. William's **CAVALRY** killed most of Harold's army. It is said that Harold II died when he was shot in the eye with an arrow, although nobody is sure if that is true.

The Bayeux (say: bye-yuh) Tapestry was a large cloth, stitched with a collection of pictures and words that show what happened when William invaded. It is a little like a comic book made of cloth, and it is around 230 feet (70 m) long!

William was crowned king on Christmas Day, 1066. He actually turned out to be a pretty good king after all.

Night Attack at Târgoviște

VLAD THE VERY NASTY MAN

Vlad the Impaler was not a nice man. He ruled Wallachia, which used to be a country in what is now eastern Europe. As a leader, he did many terrible things such as setting people on fire and boiling people in water. However, those things are nothing compared to what he did in 1462.

VLAD VS. A LOTTA OTTOMANS

Mehmed II was the ruler of the Ottoman **EMPIRE**. The Ottoman Empire was so powerful that it took money from countries around it. However, Vlad the Impaler refused to pay the money. This annoyed Mehmed quite a bit. Then Vlad invaded some Ottoman villages and killed everyone in them. This annoyed Mehmed a lot. He gathered an army of 90,000 soldiers and invaded Wallachia, heading for the capital, Târgoviște.

Vlad, meanwhile, had an army of 30,000 peasants.

Vlad was chased out of the camp.

Mehmed II and his army reached the capital city and settled down in tents, planning to attack the next day. Vlad decided to kill him in the night before his soldiers woke up. He snuck into the Ottoman camp, but he and his soldiers attacked the wrong tent!

The next morning, the Ottomans attacked Târgovişte. However, they found that the doors were open. There were no soldiers on the walls, and no Vlad to be found. They kept marching, wondering what they would find. Suddenly, in the distance they saw something. It looked like a forest of trees, but when they got closer, they realized that it was something much, much worse...

THE ROYAL COURT OF TÂRGOVIŞTE

A Nasty Way to Go

The trees were actually wooden stakes. On the stakes, Vlad had impaled dead Ottoman prisoners. This means that he stuck them on the stakes, like marshmallows on sticks. There were around 20,000 bodies, and the forest of stakes covered many **SQUARE MILES** of land. Vlad must have been collecting prisoners for a very long time. Mehmed II was so horrified and sickened by what Vlad had left for him that he took his army and marched back to Turkey, the home of the Ottoman Empire. And now you know how Vlad the Impaler got his name!

The Siege of Orleans

THE FARMER'S DAUGHTER

Joan lived on a farm in France. She looked after the animals, and learned how to sew from her mother. Joan never went too far from her home. However, in 1425, when Joan was 13, she started hearing voices from heaven telling her that she needed to help the French king and save France. Her life was about to change forever.

FRANCE WAS AT WAR, AGAIN

At the time, England and France were fighting each other in what was known as the Hundred Years' War. It had started in 1337. In Joan's lifetime, some parts of France were controlled by the French king, Charles VII, while others were controlled by the English king, Henry VI. England had been winning many important battles, and it looked like they couldn't be defeated. In 1428, when Joan was 16, the voices told her to meet the French king. She traveled to Chinon, where Charles was staying.

The English won the battle of Agincourt in 1415. Using powerful longbows, they killed many French soldiers.

LONGBOW

Can you guess how long the Hundred Years' War lasted? The answer is actually 116 years! Sometimes history just doesn't make sense!

SENT FROM GOD

When she got there, she **CONVINCED** everyone that she should be allowed to see the king. Nobody knows for sure what she said but, after the meeting, Charles believed that she had been sent by God to help him win the war against the English. He gave her armor, weapons, a horse, and a troop of soldiers.

Joan was said to be kind, as well as being a warrior.

Joan kept on winning battles until she was captured in 1430.

FIGHTING FOR FRANCE

Joan of Arc, as she was now known, had no training as a soldier at all. However, she was sent to Orleans. The city had been under **SIEGE** from the English for many months. When she got there, she was told that she had to wait for more soldiers to arrive. However, suddenly Joan decided that it was time to fight, and attacked an English fortress on the other side of the city. The French soldiers were **INSPIRED** by Joan, and together they chased the English away. Joan led the soldiers and attacked even more English fortresses around Orleans – in one battle, she was injured but carried on fighting until the French won and the city was safe.

Although Joan was captured and killed by the English, her bravery was not forgotten. She was famous throughout the land, and many historians think that she was one of the main reasons that the French won the Hundred Years' War.

The Punic Wars

Have you heard of the Romans? If you have, you probably know that they had a fearsome army full of well-trained soldiers who were killing machines. But have you ever heard about the Battle of Cannae, when the Romans completely lost? Even the Romans had bad days, and this was one of the worst...

> You can't (and didn't) win them all, Mr Roman Soldier.

LONG WARS

The Punic Wars were between the Romans and the Carthaginians (say: karth-ah-jin-ee-uns). The Carthaginians came from North Africa, while the Romans came from Europe. The two had been fighting since 264 B.C. Just before the Second Punic War started, the Carthaginians controlled parts of Spain. They had a new leader for their Spanish army. His name was Hannibal and, when he was a boy, he had sworn a **BLOOD OATH** to destroy Rome. In 216 B.C., he marched across Europe with an army, fighting any Romans that were in their way. His mission: to attack the capital, Rome.

Every date before year 0 has B.C. after it. The higher the number in a B.C. date, the further back in history it was.

```
        B.C.        A.D.

300   200   100   0   100   200   300
```

> Hannibal's army was made up of 90,000 **INFANTRY** and 12,000 cavalry. They even had a few fighting elephants. Scary!

HANNIBAL ON THE MOVE

To get to Italy, Hannibal traveled through the Alps, a mountain range in Europe. Nobody expected him to do this, and the Romans were caught by surprise. When the Carthaginians got to Italy, they won important victories in places called Trebia and Trasimene.

THE ALPS

Don't get too smug, Hannibal – the Romans eventually won the Second Punic War and kicked the Carthaginians out of Spain.

BATTLE OF CANNAE

By the time Hannibal got to the town of Cannae, he had around 40,000 infantry and 10,000 cavalry. The Romans sent an army made up of 80,000 soldiers, and 6,000 cavalry. This meant that the Roman army was nearly twice as big and it looked like they would easily win. However, Hannibal had a plan. He set his army up with his strong horsemen at the side and his weaker soldiers in the middle. When the Romans charged him, Hannibal's weaker soldiers **RETREATED**, while his horses **SURROUNDED** the enemy. The Romans were trapped! The Carthaginians slaughtered them, and Hannibal became famous for being a very clever **GENERAL**.

It is thought that around 50,000 Romans died, while the Carthaginians only lost 6,000 soldiers.

Battle of Britain

On August 20, 1940, a man named Winston Churchill made a speech. Churchill was the Prime Minister of Britain, and Britain was at war with the **NAZIS**, who were in charge of Germany. In his speech, Churchill said:

Never, in the field of human **CONFLICT**, *was so much owed by so many to so few.*

Churchill was talking about the Battle of Britain. The British air force, the RAF, and the German air force, called the Luftwaffe, fought in the skies above Britain. Everyone in Britain owed their safety to the few pilots who took to the skies in fighter planes to defend their country.

WINSTON CHURCHILL

WORLD WAR II

World War II was the biggest and deadliest war in history. The Nazis had taken over most of Europe, and Britain was one of the few countries still undefeated. The leader of the Nazis, Adolf Hitler, knew that he had to invade and destroy Britain, but there was a problem – Britain is an island. Hitler decided that he would use fighter planes to destroy the RAF and make Britain **SURRENDER**.

World War II involved people and countries from all over the world and, by the end, millions of people would be dead.

This is a Spitfire, one of the fighter planes used by the RAF.

RADAR

Although the Luftwaffe had more planes than the RAF, the British were able to use their radar systems to see when the fighter planes were coming from Germany to attack Britain. This meant they could scramble into the skies in time to defend themselves.

A WORLD WAR II RADAR DISH

A BATTLE IN THE SKY

The Battle of Britain lasted 112 days, from July 10 until October 31, 1940, according to records. It was the first all-air battle in history. Even though they were outnumbered, the RAF fended off the Luftwaffe and protected the people of Britain. As the battle progressed, the Luftwaffe began bombing cities in a period known as the Blitz. The RAF was stronger than the Germans thought, and were able to regroup and stop the Nazi attack completely. Today, the pilots who fought in the Battle of Britain are known as "The Few" because of Churchill's speech.

There were many heroes on the ground too, repairing the airplanes and finding and destroying German aeroplanes.

SUPERMARINE SPITFIRE FIGHTER PLANES IN FORMATION OVER BRITAIN.

The Napoleonic Wars

NAPOLEON WON MANY BATTLES, BOTH ON LAND AND AT SEA.

One of the greatest war generals in history was a man named Napoleon Bonaparte. He was a Frenchman famous for his clever **STRATEGIES** and important victories. He is famous for a series of wars called the Napoleonic Wars, from 1803 to 1815.

FRANCE IS ONCE AGAIN AT WAR

Napoleon went to military school, where he learned all about war. He rose through the ranks of the army and became an important soldier. Then, in 1799, he ended the French Revolution (see pages 24–25) and became leader of France. It was a messy time in French history, and Napoleon tried to make things stable again. In 1804, he made himself Emperor of France. In 1805, he defeated the Austrians and Russians and gained control of a lot of Europe. He decided that the leaders of Italy, Naples, Spain, Sweden, Holland, and Westphalia should be people that were loyal to him. This gave him even more power.

Napoleon was a busy man.

In Napoleon's time, different parts of Italy were not part of the same country. For example, Naples was separate.

18

Napoleon was loved by his soldiers.

IT ALL GOES WRONG FOR NAPOLEON

In 1806, Napoleon fought the British and, in 1807, he won against the Prussians, who signed a peace treaty – this was a piece of writing that promised that Prussia would surrender. However, soon things began to change for Napoleon. After some costly defeats, he tried to invade Russia in 1812. He completely failed, and of the 400,000 soldiers he had, fewer than 40,000 survived. The capital of France, Paris, was taken over in 1814, and Napoleon was sent away to a quiet island called Elba.

ENCORE, ENCORE

However, after less than a year, Napoleon escaped from the island and took over France again. After hearing that Napoleon was back, Britain, Russia, Prussia, and Austria declared war on him. In 1815, there was a battle near the village of Waterloo, in present-day Belgium. Napoleon was defeated and the British sent him to another faraway island called St. Helena, where he died in 1821.

ST. HELENA ISLAND

World War I

World War I was fought between 1914 and 1918. One side was mainly made up of Germany, Austria-Hungary, Bulgaria, and the Ottoman Empire, while the other side included France, Britain, Russia, Italy, and Japan. A huge number of people were involved, and as many as 8.5 million died. Lots of new **TECHNOLOGY** was invented and perfected to fight the war, such as tanks, **CHEMICAL WEAPONS**, and new machine guns. However, the war was also famous for something else: trench warfare.

WORLD WAR I
TANKS

WHAT IS TRENCH WARFARE?

Soldiers didn't get a lot of sleep. They were often woken up to do jobs or to look out for the enemy.

BRITISH SOLDIERS
IN A TRENCH

Trench warfare was fighting done in trenches. The trenches were long, narrow ditches dug in the ground. Each side would dig their own trenches on the battlefield; the land in between the trenches was called No Man's Land. Sometimes, the soldiers would charge over No Man's Land to try and take over enemy trenches. This was called "going over the top."

However, a lot of the time, not much happened while living in a trench. In fact, enemy soldiers weren't the only thing to worry about for men in the trenches. The trenches were muddy and smelly. Toilets overflowed, dead bodies lay nearby, and there were rats and lice everywhere.

TRENCH FOOT

TRENCH FOOT

155. Waldron. 62. Trench Feet. 29.11.16

Many soldiers got an **INFECTION** called trench foot. It was caused by standing in cold, wet mud for hours and hours. The blood would stop going to their feet, and sometimes their socks would even become attached to their skin. In very bad cases, they would have to have their foot or their leg cut off by a doctor.

SHELL SHOCK

Shell shock was an illness that affected the mind. Being around explosions, gunfire, and danger could affect soldiers **PERMANENTLY**. It could cause nightmares and make men tired and confused. Sometimes soldiers would shake all the time, or not be able to eat. Many officers didn't believe that shell shock was a real illness, so they forced soldiers to keep fighting.

It is called shell shock because the explosives fired at the soldiers were called shells.

On Christmas Day, 1914, a lot of the soldiers on both sides called an unofficial **TRUCE** and stopped fighting. They gave each other gifts and some even played football in No Man's Land.

21

The Battle of Cajamarca

ATAHUALPA THE INCA

In 1532, Atahualpa became leader of the Incas. He had just won a war against his half-brother and was waiting for him to be brought to the town of Cajamarca. Atahualpa and his people were **FASTING** as part of their **RELIGION** when they heard about a small group of Spanish soldiers in their lands. However, the Inca leader was surrounded by thousands of well-trained soldiers, and he was not worried about a few enemies. He decided to ignore them.

The Incas lived in South America, in and around a mountain range called the Andes. It is the longest mountain range on land.

Statue of Atahualpa

PIZARRO THE SPANIARD

Meanwhile, the Spanish soldiers continued their travels. They were led by a man named Pizarro. He had heard that there was a rich empire nearby, and he was determined to find it and take whatever treasure he could. Although Pizarro had fewer than 200 soldiers, they had guns and horses, which many of the Inca people had never even seen before. Pizarro and his men formed a plan to capture Atahualpa.

SPANISH BETRAYAL

In November, the Spanish finally turned up at Cajamarca. Atahualpa agreed to meet with them at the town square. Pizarro hid his cannons and horses behind buildings and waited. Atahualpa had 80,000 soldiers, but he left most of them outside the town. When the Incas got there, the Spanish handed them a prayer book and told them about God. However, Atahualpa threw it away in disgust – the Incas had their own religion!

Suddenly Pizarro called his cannons, horses, and soldiers out and opened fire. In the space of two hours, thousands and thousands of Incas were killed. During the battle, Atahualpa was captured. Pizarro made the Incas pay a huge ransom to save their leader. However, after they gave the Spanish a room full of gold and silver, Pizarro went back on his word. He killed the Inca leader by burning him at the stake!

Shame on you, Pizarro!

Atahualpa only took 5,000 unarmed soldiers and noblemen with him to meet the Spanish.

Not a single Spanish soldier was killed in the battle. In fact, the only Spanish person who was injured was Pizarro – he cut his hand as he captured Atahualpa.

The French Revolution

Not all wars are between different countries. Sometimes a country can have a war with itself. This is called a civil war, or a revolution. One of the nastiest revolutions was the French Revolution. At the end of the 18th century, there were three different groups of people in France, called estates:

1. The first estate was made up of the clergy. These were people who worked for the church.

2. The second estate was made up of the nobles. These were kings, queens, and other important people.

3. The third estate was made up of the peasants. They were farmers and workers, and they were often poor. Even though most people were part of the peasant class, the clergy and nobles had all the power. This was very unfair and, in 1789, the third estate decided to do something about it.

The peasants had to pay all of the **TAXES**, and the nobles had all of the good jobs. The nobles also got to wear very fancy clothes.

AN UPRISING

The peasants stormed a fortress called the Bastille to steal gunpowder and weapons. This was the start of the French Revolution. Fear spread through the country like wildfire. Soon, all the peasants were arming themselves. They burned down the houses of tax collectors and rich people. Eventually, the third estate took over the country.

THE REIGN OF TERROR

However, in 1793, the revolution became much nastier. The revolutionaries, led by a man named Robespierre, arrested the king and said he was guilty of **TREASON**. They **BEHEADED** the king using a guillotine. Nine months later, the last queen of France, Marie Antoinette, was killed in the same way. Soon, anyone who disagreed with the revolution was guillotined.

This is a guillotine. The person kneels down with their head poking through the hole, and a giant blade comes down and chops their head off.

THE REVOLUTIONARY WARS

Revolutionaries also started wars with other countries, called the Revolutionary Wars. Robespierre and his people wanted to spread their ideas to other countries. They thought that peasants across Europe should rise up and fight. During this time, many prisoners of the Revolution were murdered by some revolutionaries. This was known as the September Massacre. It was at this point that people started to wonder if this had all gone too far...

Robespierre was sent to the guillotine in 1794 by people who thought he was no longer a good leader. Better late than never.

Over 17,000 people were recorded as being executed by the guillotine during the Revolution. However, there may have been many more that weren't recorded.

In 1799, the French Revolution ended after a man named Napoleon took control and said he was leader of France. But the Revolution had changed France forever. The nobles were gone, and the clergy had much less power.

The Great Emu War

After World War I, thousands of Australian soldiers had returned home to find that they couldn't get another job. The government decided that they would offer these soldiers homes and farms all over the country. However, farming in Australia was difficult at the time, especially when growing wheat. The biggest problem wasn't droughts or money problems. It was emus.

The Greatest Enemy

AN ARMY OF EMUS

Emus are giant, flightless birds. There were about 20,000 of them in Australia at the time. They roamed the country, eating wheat and tearing down fences. The farmers had tried to deal with the emus themselves but had to give up. The emus were too strong. In 1932, the farmers asked the government for help. It was time to declare war on the emus.

Emus are about 5.7 feet (1.75 m) tall. They are the second-largest living bird.

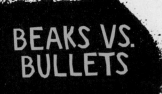

BEAKS VS. BULLETS

The Australians sent a small group of soldiers to kill the birds. The force was led by Major G.P.W. Meredith. They were armed with machine guns and over 10,000 bullets. However, the first day of battle went very badly for the Australians. As soon as they opened fire, the giant birds scattered in all directions. The animals were much smarter and faster than the soldiers expected!

This is a Lewis gun, which the Australian army used against the emus.

RETREAT!

On the second day, the soldiers ambushed the emus. However, even though they fired hundreds and hundreds of bullets, fewer than 12 emus were killed. It seemed that the soldiers would never be able to win. Soon the newspapers began reporting on the Great Emu War. The government began to get scared that this would get very embarrassing for them, so they told their soldiers to come home. The farmers, who were still having problems with the emus, begged the government to send more soldiers. But they said no. The emus had won.

EMUS CELEBRATE VICTORY

It reportedly took 10 bullets to bring down a single emu.

The Battle of Thermopylae

In 480 B.C., Xerxes, the king of Persia, invaded Greece. Persia had a huge empire, with massive armies, and Xerxes wanted more land. However, in Greece, the Athenians and the city-state of Sparta would not give in to Persia. They were ready to protect their country. The Greek army was mostly made up of Spartans – they were fierce and terrifying warriors. Their leader was a man named Leonidas.

Xerxes told the Spartans to give up their weapons. The Spartans, who were ready for a fight, told him to "come and take them."

Xerxes's father, Darius I, sent messengers to Athens and Sparta, telling them to peacefully accept the Persians as their rulers. The Greeks were so angry that they threw the messengers into pits.

TO THE HOT GATES!

The Greeks were completely outnumbered. They only had around 7,000 soldiers, while Xerxes had an army between 70,000 and 300,000. Leonidas knew that the best place to fight the Persians was an area called Thermopylae. This meant "The Hot Gates" in Greek. Thermopylae was perfect because it was a stretch of narrow land next to the sea. This meant that the Persian forces couldn't surround the Greeks. Their bigger army would be useless.

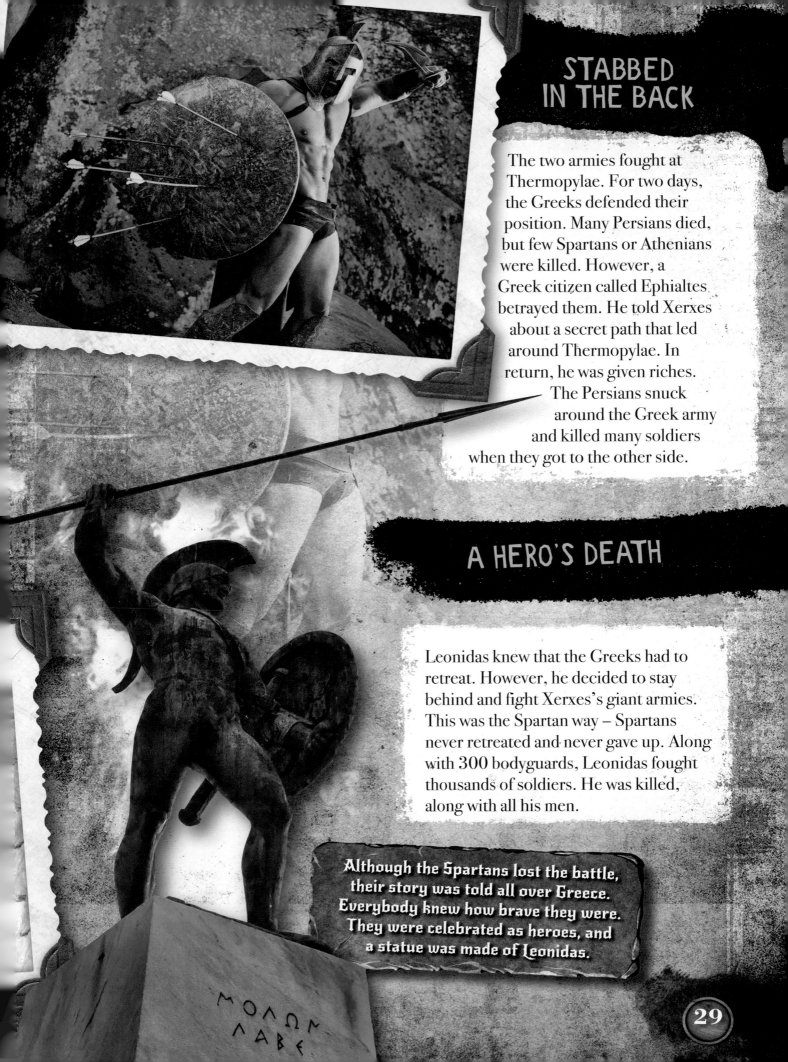

STABBED IN THE BACK

The two armies fought at Thermopylae. For two days, the Greeks defended their position. Many Persians died, but few Spartans or Athenians were killed. However, a Greek citizen called Ephialtes betrayed them. He told Xerxes about a secret path that led around Thermopylae. In return, he was given riches. The Persians snuck around the Greek army and killed many soldiers when they got to the other side.

A HERO'S DEATH

Leonidas knew that the Greeks had to retreat. However, he decided to stay behind and fight Xerxes's giant armies. This was the Spartan way – Spartans never retreated and never gave up. Along with 300 bodyguards, Leonidas fought thousands of soldiers. He was killed, along with all his men.

Although the Spartans lost the battle, their story was told all over Greece. Everybody knew how brave they were. They were celebrated as heroes, and a statue was made of Leonidas.

Mystery Solved?

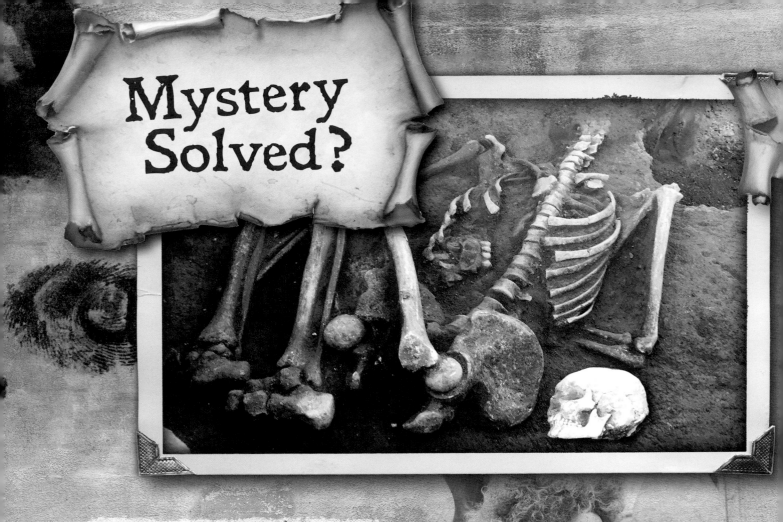

Did you find any war that would explain our skeleton, here in the museum? If you said the French Revolution, well done! Thousands of people had their heads chopped off in this war, just like this skeleton has. France is in Europe, which was where this skeleton was found.

Perhaps this person was a rich nobleman in France. For years he might have had piles of treasure and money. Maybe he laughed at the peasants, and then went off to party in a big mansion. What did he do when the third estate took over the country? Did this nobleman try to run away? Did he pretend to be poor? One thing is for sure, he found himself in front of the guillotine eventually. Before he knew it, his head was rolling around on the floor alongside those of the king and queen of France. If this is true, it would just be one of the many stories that survive through time and history and teach us about the past.

Glossary

ANCIENT belonging to the very distant past and no longer in existence

BEHEADED when someone's head is chopped off

BLOOD OATH a strong agreement, where both people cut their palms and shake hands

CAVALRY the parts of an army that serve on horseback

CHEMICAL WEAPONS weapons, such as gases and sprays, that cause harm to humans using chemicals

CHRISTIANS people who believe in the religion of Christianity

CONFLICT active disagreement between people

CONVINCED made people believe something

DEFEATED beaten or lost

EMPIRE a group of countries or nations under one ruler

FASTING not eating or drinking, usually for religious reasons

GENERAL the leader of an army

INFANTRY the parts of an army that serve on foot

INFECTION an illness caused by dirt, germs, and bacteria getting into the body

INSPIRED created a feeling in other people in which they believed they could do something great

MUSLIMS people who follow the religion of Islam

NAZIS a group of people that controlled Germany from 1933 to 1945 and fought in World War II

NOBLEMAN a person who is part of the highest social class

PERMANENTLY lasting forever

RELIGION the belief in and worship of a god or gods

REMAINS parts that have been left behind; of a building, artifact, or body

RETREATED ran away

SIEGE when a town or building is surrounded and attacked for a long time

SQUARE MILES measurements of areas that are squares with each side being a mile in length

STRATEGIES plans or actions with overall long-term military goals in mind

SURRENDER to stop fighting an enemy and submit to their authority

SURROUNDED enclosed on all sides

TAXES payments made to the government so that they can provide services

TECHNOLOGY machines or devices that are made using scientific knowledge

TREASON a crime in which someone betrays their country

TRUCE a break in a conflict where both sides agree not to fight

Index